11·8·79

John Clancy's Fish Cookery

PREVIOUS BOOKS
BY JOHN CLANCY:

The John Clancy Baking Book

Clancy's Oven Cookery
John Clancy & Frances Field

JOHN CLANCY'S FISH COOKERY

by John Clancy

with Beatrice Saunders

Illustrations by Suzanne Dahlquist

HOLT, RINEHART AND WINSTON · NEW YORK

Published by Holt, Rinehart and Winston, 383 Madison
Avenue, New York, New York 10017.

Published simultaneously in Canada by Holt, Rinehart
and Winston of Canada, Limited.

Library of Congress Cataloging in Publication Data
Clancy, John.
    John Clancy's Fish cookery.
    Includes index.
    1. Cookery (Fish) I. Saunders, Beatrice, joint
author. II. Title. III. Title: Fish cookery.
TX747.C57   641.6′9   79-4044
ISBN Hardbound: 0-03-047446-9
ISBN Paperback: 0-03-047451-5
First Edition

Designer: Amy Hill
Printed in the United States of America
10 9 8 7 6 5 4 3 2 1

In memory of my father, an ardent fisherman, and for my mother, who turned his catches into a feast.

Contents

Preface   xi

On Buying Fish, Shellfish, and Crustaceans   xiii

Broiling

SALMON STEAKS   2

FISH TERIYAKI   3

KING CRAB LEGS   4

SHRIMP ON A SKEWER   6

CLAMS WITH HERBED BUTTER   8

OYSTERS WITH HERBED BUTTER   10

LOBSTERS STUFFED WITH SHRIMP   12

Baking

BLUEFISH OR STRIPED BASS
BAKED FISH WITH ONIONS AND TOMATOES   16

RED SNAPPER OR BLUEFISH
WITH CITRUS FRUIT JUICES   17

STUFFED SHRIMP   18

STUFFED STRIPED BASS   20

OYSTERS ROCKEFELLER   21

DEVILED CRABS   23

MOUSSE OF SOLE   24

Steaming

CLAMS 28

OYSTERS 29

MUSSELS 30

STUFFED LOBSTER WITH COGNAC 31

Deep-Fat Frying

DEEP-FRIED FISH IN BATTER
SOLE, HADDOCK, FLOUNDER, COD, OCEAN PERCH,
OR ANY WHITE-MEAT FISH 34

BATTER-FRIED SHRIMP 36

OYSTERS IN BATTER 38

CODFISH BALLS 40

SOFT-SHELL CRABS 42

Sautéing

CRAB MEAT SAUTÉ 46

SCAMPI 47

CRAB CAKES 49

SOLE MEUNIÈRE
(ALSO FLOUNDER OR OCEAN PERCH) 51

BROOK TROUT AMANDINE 52

SOFT-SHELL CRABS MEUNIÈRE 54

SCALLOPS PROVENÇALE 56

Poaching

    CODFISH, HADDOCK, OR SALMON STEAKS   60

    STRIPED BASS   61

    OCEAN PERCH FLORENTINE   63

Sauces

    AÏOLI   66

    BÉARNAISE   66

    CURRY   67

    EGG AND TOMATO   69

    FISH STOCK   70

    HERBED BUTTER   71

    HOLLANDAISE   71

    MAYONNAISE   72

    MOUSSELINE   73

    MUSTARD   74

    NANTUA   74

    RÉMOULADE   76

    BEURRE BLANC   76

    TARTAR   77

    WHITE WINE   78

Preface

I have lived close to the sea all my life. When I was a child, in eastern Long Island, fishing trips with my father were a regular weekend treat. And that was preceded by the excitement of finding bait—coaxing fiddler crabs out of the sand tunnels in the nearby saltwater marshes and digging out clams from the beach in front of the house.

We would set out, my father and I, in our dory at five or six in the morning, when the tide was right. At the end of the day there was always a sumptuous feast at home, whether a hefty chowder, baked bluefish, or striped bass. Or, if it was before 1938, mussels steamed in a mixture of white wine, onions, thyme, and freshly ground pepper. In 1938 a hurricane (at that time hurricanes carried no names) destroyed the mussel beds for years to come. They have not yet reappeared.

In time my father acquired a larger vessel, and we were able to venture out for lobsters. Lobster pots were primitive then—wooden crates nailed to a wooden frame, with an opening on hinges. What glee when the pots were hauled up from the bottom, forty or so feet below, teeming with lobsters; and what anticipation we felt looking forward to the tastes of a delicious stew or one of my mother's specialties—stuffed lobster—broiled to perfection.

By age seventeen I was an experienced fisherman, working with my father on his boat for hire and catering fishing parties for up to fifty people at a time, at one of which the largest fluke on record was hauled up from the bottom of the Sound. It was over sixteen pounds and a perfect "doormat," so called because of the shape of this oversized summer flounder. What an eating experience it made—filleted, poached, and served with a mustard sauce.

My early experiences have led me naturally into the food world. And my life at and near the sea has given me a keen understanding of fish and its preparation. In the course of time I improved on the dishes of early memory and added to my storehouse those I came upon subsequently, either in their original form or refined to suit my taste. Assembled here in this book are forty-nine recipes that I would like to share with you.

At one time fish and seafood were locally found and locally

consumed. Today freshwater and saltwater fish are transported everywhere and are available throughout the country. Frozen fish can also be bought nearly everywhere.

I think of this book not as a collection of recipes so much as an attempt to put into print the kind of instruction readers would receive if they were attending my classes in fish cookery. The step-by-step instructions, accompanied by illustrations, take my place as teacher. The format is designed to help you organize yourself in the kitchen. And the recipes are the vehicles for teaching cooking techniques, the same way that I do in the class sessions. The emphasis is on teaching basic *methods* and on understanding useful cooking *principles*. If the student could learn all he or she needs to know just by reading a recipe, there would be no need for teachers or demonstrations.

Recipes for suggested sauces appear at the end of the book.

Before starting, check the list of ingredients to make sure everything is on hand. Follow the suggested order. You will find the task simplified and your cooking pleasure greatly enhanced if you follow the instructions closely.

And now you are ready to enjoy cooking and eating the food that has been an exciting part of my life.

JOHN CLANCY

On Buying Fish, Shellfish, and Crustaceans

It is a maxim in cooking that a dish can only be as good as its ingredients. The most enticing-sounding and best-written recipe cannot disguise poor ingredients. Following are what I consider to be the basic tips on buying fish, shellfish, and crustaceans. They will help produce the rewards that your palate deserves.

1. The flesh of fresh fish should be firm and should spring back when you press down on it with your fingers. If the flesh remains dented, the fish is not fresh.

2. The scales should be shiny and tightly attached to the skin.

3. The gills need to be red or clear pink; a brownish coloring is the result of stale blood.

4. The eyes should be bulging and clear; a milky film, or worse, eyes that are sunken into their sockets, are sure indicators of a fish that has had its day.

5. Saltwater fish should have the "smell of the sea." Freshwater fish should not have a brackish odor. Neither should yield a "fishy" redolence.

6. "Fresh frozen" fillets are perfectly fit for any recipe in the book. Once defrosted, however, they must not be refrozen. Buyer's note: Icy crystals on frozen fish indicate that the fish has been refrozen.

7. Fresh fish fillets should be almost odorless and free of slime.

8. Fresh lobsters and crabs must be alive when you buy them.

9. The best way to check crab meat for freshness is to run your fingertip over it; it should not be "slick," but instead should feel almost dry.

10. Clams, oysters, and mussels should be tightly closed and feel heavy for their size. This indicates plumpness and the presence of plenty of liquid, both desirable qualities. When you knock two together, they should not sound hollow.

11. Scallops need to be firm. They can be pinkish, white, or white with a yellow hue. The older they are, the more gray or colorless they tend to be and the more "milky" their liquid.

12. Shrimp must be firm and almost odor-free, but the "smell of the sea" is as desirable for shrimp as it is for fresh saltwater fish.

The smell of your fish market can be the best indicator of the quality of the ingredients you use in cooking fish.

BROILING

SALMON STEAKS

(Serves 4)

INGREDIENTS

4   salmon steaks, 8 to 10 ounces each

4   tablespoons unsalted butter
     vegetable oil
1   teaspoon salt
1   lemon

Suggested Sauces

Herbed Garlic Butter
Béarnaise

HOW TO PROCEED

· Melt butter in small saucepan and set aside.
· Assemble ingredients and prepare sauce of
    your choice.
· Preheat broiler and place oven rack 4 inches
    from heat.
· Lightly grease broiler pan with vegetable
    oil.
· Place salmon steaks on broiler pan.
· Brush steaks with melted butter and sprin-
    kle with salt.
· Broil steaks for about 3 minutes on each
    side, or until fish flakes easily when
    tested with a fork.

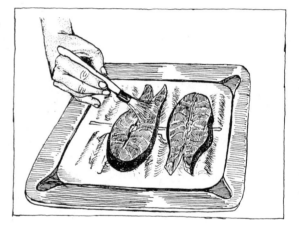

· Transfer steaks to serving platter and re-
    move skin.
· Serve with sauce of your choice or lemon,
    cut into wedges.

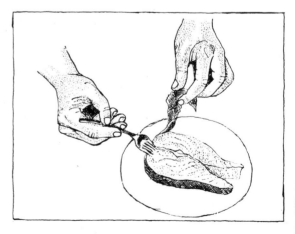

FISH TERIYAKI

(Serves 4)

INGREDIENTS

2 to 2½ pounds fillets of fish (red snapper,
     porgy, striped bass, or bluefish)
2   teaspoons dry mustard
1   teaspoon hot water
1   teaspoon cornstarch
2   tablespoons dry sherry
¼   cup Japanese soy sauce
½   cup chicken broth
1   tablespoon sugar
    vegetable oil

HOW TO PROCEED

· Wash fish under cold running water.
· Pat dry with paper towels.
· Mix mustard with hot water and let sit for
    10 minutes.
· Dissolve cornstarch in sherry in small cup
    and set aside.
· Combine mustard mixture, soy sauce,
    chicken broth, and sugar in small sauce-
    pan.
· Bring mixture to a simmer over medium
    heat.
· Stir sherry and cornstarch, and add to soy
    sauce mixture, stirring constantly, until
    mixture thickens slightly and becomes
    clear.
· Remove from heat.
· Preheat broiler and place oven rack 4 inches
    from heat.
· Lightly grease broiler pan with vegetable
    oil.
· Place fillets on pan, skin side down.
· Brush fish with soy sauce mixture and broil
    for 16 to 18 minutes. Fillet size deter-
    mines broiling time.

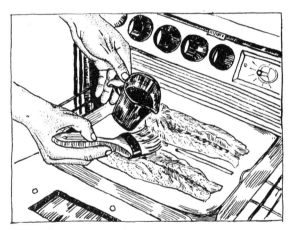

· Brush intermittently with soy sauce mix-
    ture, or until fish flakes easily when
    tested with a fork.
· Just before serving, pour a little soy sauce
    mixture over each fillet.

KING CRAB LEGS

(Serves 4)

INGREDIENTS

4	frozen king crab legs, 10 to 12 ounces each, thawed
½	pound (2 sticks) unsalted butter
½	teaspoon dried tarragon
2	tablespoons lemon juice
1	tablespoon Worcestershire sauce
¼	cup dry white wine
1	teaspoon salt
½	teaspoon freshly ground black pepper

HOW TO PROCEED

· Preheat broiler and place oven rack 4 inches from heat.
· With large kitchen or poultry shears, cut crab legs into 4- to 6-inch sections.

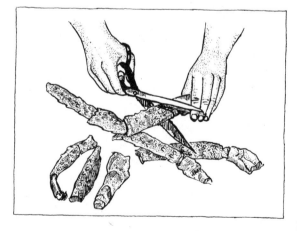

- Make two parallel cuts a half inch apart through length of shell and remove cut section of shell.
- Melt butter in small saucepan.
- Add tarragon, lemon juice, Worcestershire sauce, white wine, salt, and pepper.

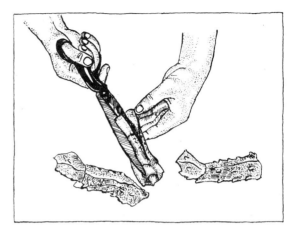

- Place crab legs, cut side up, on broiler pan. Brush crab legs with butter mixture.
- Broil for 8 to 10 minutes, basting with butter mixture intermittently.
- Serve leftover butter mixture in small cups as dipping sauce.

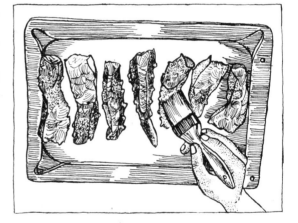

SHRIMP ON A SKEWER

(Serves 4)

INGREDIENTS

2   dozen jumbo shrimp

FOR MARINADE
¼   cup coarsely chopped flat-leaf parsley
1   cup olive oil
½   teaspoon freshly ground black pepper
2   teaspoons finely chopped garlic
1   teaspoon salt
½   teaspoon dried oregano
½   cup dry white wine
2   tablespoons lemon juice

HOW TO PROCEED

· Two hours ahead of when you plan to serve,
place paring knife against underside of
shrimp and pull shell toward you and
away from flesh of shrimp, leaving last
section of shell and tail intact.

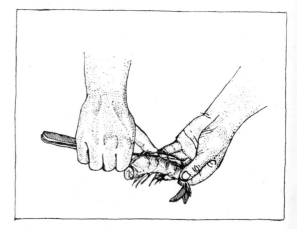

· Place shrimp on its side, with back facing
   you. Cut shrimp, ¼ inch deep, down the
   back, stopping at portion of shell that remains intact.
· Devein shrimp by washing under cold running water.
· Pat dry with paper towels.
· Mix all ingredients for marinade in bowl
   large enough to hold shrimp.
· Place shrimp in marinade, turning once or
   twice, to coat evenly.
· Refrigerate for 2 hours.

· Preheat broiler and place oven rack 4 inches
   from heat.

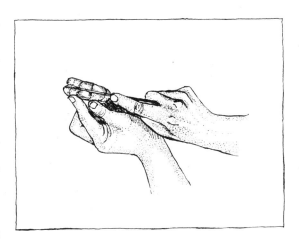

· Thread six shrimp onto each of four skewers
   by inserting tip of skewer through center
   of shrimp.
· Place on broiling pan. Broil for 6 minutes,
   turn shrimp, and continue to broil for 6
   minutes longer, or until shrimp are firm
   to the touch.
· Use marinade to baste the shrimp while
   broiling and also as dipping sauce.

CLAMS WITH HERBED BUTTER

(Serves 4)

INGREDIENTS

2   dozen littleneck clams, in their shells

¼   pound (1 stick) unsalted butter, softened
2   tablespoons chopped parsley
½   teaspoon dried oregano
1   teaspoon Worcestershire sauce
½   teaspoon salt
½   teaspoon freshly ground black pepper
½   teaspoon chopped garlic
½   cup fresh bread crumbs

HOW TO PROCEED

· In small bowl, mash butter with wooden
  spoon until soft.
· Mix in parsley, oregano, Worcestershire
  sauce, salt, pepper, and garlic. Refrigerate until chilled.
· Shape chilled butter mixture into roll 1 inch
  in diameter and about 7 inches long.
· Wrap in waxed paper, return to refrigerator, and chill for about 1 hour or until
  very firm.

TO SHUCK CLAMS
· Wash clams thoroughly under cold running
  water.
· With left hand, hold clam in crook of thumb,
  hinge side down.
· Place clam knife between halves of shell.
· Position thumb against narrow end of clam.

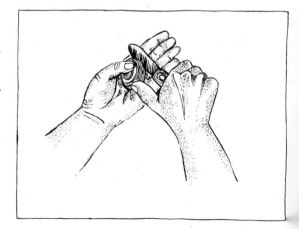

· Using pressure of the four fingers of left
  hand, push knife into clam, dividing
  shells. Discard top shell.
· Cut both muscles from the bottom halves of
  shells to free clams.
· Divide "clams on the half shell" evenly and
  place in four baking dishes.

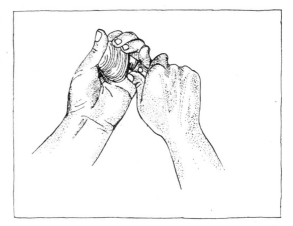

· Preheat broiler and place oven rack 4 inches
  from heat.
· Cut butter into ¼-inch slices. Place one slice
  on each clam.
· Sprinkle bread crumbs on top of butter.
  Place clams under broiler for 3 to 4 minutes, or until butter is bubbling and
  crumbs are golden brown.

OYSTERS WITH HERBED BUTTER

(Serves 4)

INGREDIENTS

2   dozen oysters in their shells

½   pound (2 sticks) unsalted butter,
         softened
4   tablespoons chopped parsley
½   teaspoon dried oregano
1½ teaspoons Worcestershire sauce
1   teaspoon salt
½   teaspoon freshly ground black pepper
1   teaspoon finely chopped garlic
1   cup fresh bread crumbs

HOW TO PROCEED

· In medium-size bowl, mash butter with
   wooden spoon until soft.
· Mix in parsley, oregano, Worcestershire
   sauce, salt, pepper, and garlic. Refrigerate.
· Shape chilled butter mixture into roll 2
   inches in diameter and about 7 inches
   long.
· Wrap in waxed paper, return to refrigerator, and chill for about 1 hour or until
   very firm.

TO SHUCK OYSTERS
· Wash oysters thoroughly under cold running water.
· Hold narrow end of oyster between thumb
   and fingers, flat side up. To separate
   shells, insert point of oyster knife near
   narrow end where shells are joined.

· Cut muscle attached to flat upper shell, then
  cut around rim.
· Remove top shell.
· Separate oyster from shell by cutting loose
  bottom portion of muscle attached to deep
  half of shell.
· Divide "oysters on the half shell" evenly and
  place in four baking dishes.

· Preheat broiler and place oven rack 4 inches
  from heat.
· Cut butter into ¼-inch slices. Place one slice
  on each oyster.
· Sprinkle bread crumbs on top of butter.
· Place oysters under broiler for 3 to 4 minutes, or until butter is bubbling and
  crumbs are golden brown.

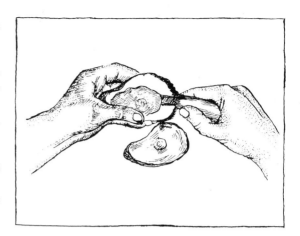

LOBSTERS STUFFED WITH SHRIMP

(Serves 4)

INGREDIENTS

4   live lobsters, 1½ to 1¾ pounds each

FOR STUFFING
4   shrimp, peeled and deveined (see p. 6
        for how to peel and devein shrimp)
24   saltine crackers
¼   pound (1 stick) unsalted butter
½   cup chopped flat-leaf parsley
1   teaspoon chopped garlic
2   tablespoons dry sherry
½   teaspoon freshly ground black pepper
½   pound (2 sticks) unsalted butter
1   lemon

HOW TO PROCEED

· Place lobsters on their backs. With large,
  heavy sharp knife and mallet, split them
  in half lengthwise. Crack large claws
  with back of knife.

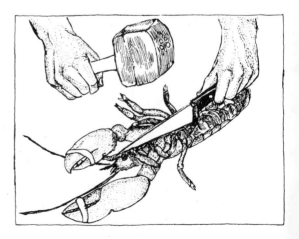

· Remove sac and intestinal vein.

TO MAKE STUFFING
· Finely chop shrimp.
· Place saltines in medium-size bowl. With
    hands or wooden spoon, crush them into
    coarse crumbs.
· Melt ¼ pound butter in a small saucepan
    and add to crumbs, along with parsley,
    garlic, sherry, pepper, and chopped
    shrimp.
· Mix well and set aside in refrigerator.

· Melt ½ pound butter and keep warm on very
    low heat.
· Preheat broiler and place oven rack 4 inches
    from heat.
· Brush lobster meat with a little of the
    melted butter; sprinkle lightly with salt.
· Place lobsters on broiling pan, flesh side up,
    and broil for 12 minutes. Remove from
    broiler.
· Dividing it evenly, place stuffing in center
    section of each lobster.
· Return lobsters to broiler and continue to
    broil for additional 4 to 6 minutes, or un-
    til stuffing is golden brown.
  Serve with remaining melted butter and
    lemon, cut into wedges.

BAKING

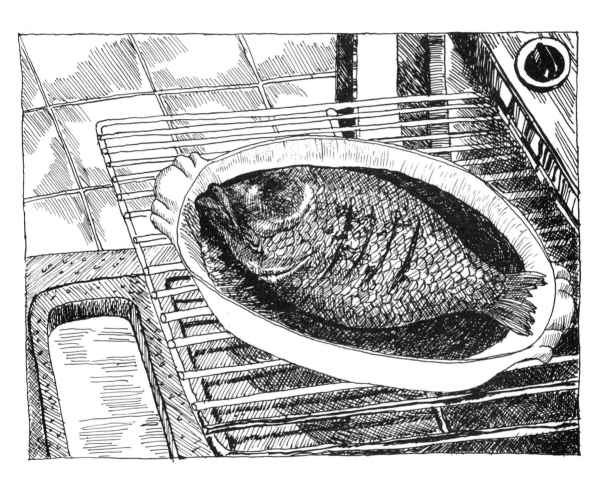

BLUEFISH OR STRIPED BASS

(BAKED FISH WITH ONIONS AND TOMATOES)
(Serves 4)

INGREDIENTS

2 to 2½ pounds fillets of bluefish or striped
     bass
4   tablespoons vegetable oil
1   teaspoon salt
½   teaspoon freshly ground black pepper
1   large onion, sliced very thin
1   large tomato, cut into slices ⅛ inch
    thick
2   tablespoons chopped parsley

HOW TO PROCEED

· Wash fish under cold running water.
· Pat dry with paper towels.
· Preheat oven to 350° F. Place oven rack in
   middle position.
· With 1 tablespoon oil, grease a baking dish
   large enough to hold fillets in one layer.
· Place fish, skin side down, in dish and sprin-
   kle with half the salt and pepper.
· Place onion and tomato slices, overlapping
   them, on top of fillets.
· Season with remaining salt and pepper.
· Dribble remaining oil on top of tomatoes
   and onions.
· Bake fish for 14 to 16 minutes, or until fish
   flakes easily when tested with a fork.
· Sprinkle fish with parsley.

RED SNAPPER OR BLUEFISH

(WITH CITRUS FRUIT JUICES)
(Serves 4)

INGREDIENTS

3 to 3½ pounds red snapper, cleaned, with
     head and tail left on
1   cup fresh orange juice
2   tablespoons lemon juice
2   limes
1½ teaspoons salt
½   teaspoon freshly ground black pepper
1   cup finely chopped onions
2   tablespoons chopped parsley

HOW TO PROCEED

· Wash fish inside and out under cold running
    water.
· Pat dry with paper towels.
· Combine orange and lemon juices in a cup.
· Cut each lime into four wedges for garnish
    and set aside in refrigerator.
· Make four slashes on each side of fish.
· Rub fish inside and out with salt and pep-
    per.
· Scatter ½ cup onions on bottom of large,
    shallow baking dish.
· Place fish on top of onions and pour orange
    and lemon juices over fish.
· Scatter remaining onions on top of fish.
· Let fish sit for 30 minutes.
· Preheat oven to 400° F.
· Bake fish for 30 minutes, or until flesh
    flakes easily when tested with a fork.
· Sprinkle with chopped parsley.
· Serve with lime wedges and juices remain-
    ing in baking dish.

STUFFED SHRIMP

(Serves 4)

INGREDIENTS

28 jumbo shrimp (10 to 14 shrimp per
        pound), peeled and deveined, with
        tails left on (see page 6 for how to
        peel and devein shrimp)
24 saltine crackers
½   pound (2 sticks) unsalted butter
½   cup chopped flat-leaf parsley
1   teaspoon chopped garlic
2   tablespoons dry sherry
½   teaspoon freshly ground black pepper
4   lemon wedges

HOW TO PROCEED

TO MAKE STUFFING
· Finely chop four shrimp.
· Place saltines in medium-size bowl. With
    hands or wooden spoon, crush them into
    coarse crumbs.
· Melt 1 stick butter in small saucepan and
    add to crumbs, along with parsley, garlic,
    sherry, pepper, and chopped shrimp.
· Mix well and set aside in refrigerator.

· To butterfly shrimp, cut down the back,
    reaching almost all the way through un-
    derside.
· Preheat oven to 400° F.

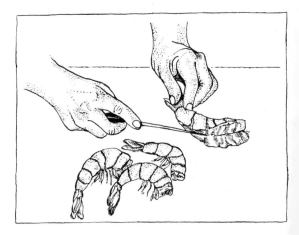

· With shrimp, cut side down, place 1 heaping
    tablespoon stuffing on top of each shrimp.
· Shape into a mound.

· With fingers, open tail fins and press them
    over stuffing.
· Place stuffed shrimp in ovenproof dish.
· Bake for 10 minutes.
· Melt remaining 1 stick butter while shrimp
    are baking.
· Serve with melted butter and lemon
    wedges.

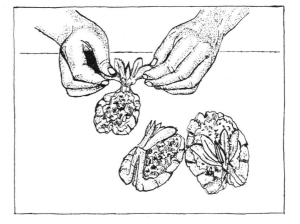

STUFFED STRIPED BASS

(Serves 4)

INGREDIENTS

4 to 4½ pounds striped bass, cleaned, with
     head and tail left on
1   cup fresh lump crab meat
6 to 8 saltine crackers
¼   pound (1 stick) unsalted butter, melted
3   tablespoons lemon juice
1½ teaspoons salt
2   teaspoons freshly ground black pepper
¼   cup chopped celery
¼   cup chopped scallions
2   tablespoons chopped green pepper
2   tablespoons chopped parsley
½   teaspoon dry mustard
½   cup dry white wine or vermouth

HOW TO PROCEED

· Wash fish inside and out under cold running
    water.
· Pat dry with paper towels.

TO MAKE STUFFING
· Flake crab meat and remove any cartilage.
· In medium-size bowl, with hands or wooden
    spoon, crush saltines into coarse crumbs.
· Stir in half the melted butter, 2 tablespoons
    lemon juice, 1 teaspoon salt, 1½ tea-
    spoons pepper, and celery, scallions,
    green pepper, parsley, and dry mustard.

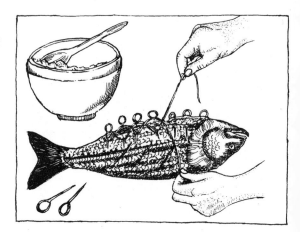

· Preheat oven to 400° F.
· Add wine or vermouth to remaining 4 ta-
    blespoons melted butter.
· Make three slashes on each side of fish.
· Rub inside and out with remaining lemon
    juice.
· Sprinkle with remaining ½ teaspoon salt
    and pepper.

· Fill cavity of fish with stuffing.
· Sew fish closed with white thread or secure
    with small skewers and place in large
    baking dish.
· Pour butter-wine mixture over fish.
· Bake for 30 minutes, basting two or three
    times intermittently.
· Serve with liquid from the pan.

OYSTERS ROCKEFELLER

(Serves 4)

INGREDIENTS

2   dozen oysters, on the half shell (see p.
        10 for how to shuck oysters)

2   packages frozen spinach, 10 ounces each
4   tablespoons (½ stick) unsalted butter
½   cup finely chopped onions
2   teaspoons finely chopped garlic
½   cup chopped scallions
¼   cup finely chopped parsley
1   tablespoon Worcestershire sauce
¾ to 1 cup clam juice
¼   teaspoon cayenne pepper
    salt

HOW TO PROCEED

· Cook spinach according to directions on
    package.
· When spinach is done, immediately plunge
    it into cold water.
· Place cooled spinach in wire strainer.
· Remove water from spinach by pressing
    against inside of strainer with back of
    wooden spoon.

  Melt butter in large skillet.
  Sauté onions in butter over medium heat
      until transparent.
  Add garlic and scallions and cook for 1 min-
      ute more, stirring all the while.
  Remove from heat and stir in spinach, pars-
      ley, and Worcestershire sauce.

· Place oven rack in middle position and pre-
heat oven to 400° F.
· Place half spinach mixture in container of
electric blender.
· Add about ¼ cup clam juice.
· Blend at high speed for 1 minute, or until
mixture becomes a smooth purée.
· Add additional clam juice if necessary.
· Repeat this process with remaining mix-
ture.*
· Add cayenne pepper and taste for salt.
· Spoon mixture evenly over oysters and
place in large baking pan.
· Bake oysters for 15 minutes, or until top-
ping is lightly browned.

*When using food processor, place *all* the spinach
in container of processor and *omit* clam juice.

DEVILED CRABS

(Serves 4)

INGREDIENTS

1   pound fresh lump crab meat or 1 pound
       frozen king crab meat, thawed
8   saltines
¼   pound (1 stick) unsalted butter
¼   cup dry sherry
½   cup finely chopped celery
2   tablespoons finely chopped green pepper
½   cup finely chopped scallions
½   cup coarsely chopped flat-leaf parsley
¼   teaspoon cayenne pepper
      salt

HOW TO PROCEED

· Preheat oven to 350° F.
· Flake crab meat and remove any cartilage.
· Press excess liquid through strainer with
     back of wooden spoon and discard.
· Crumble saltines with hands into large
     bowl.
· Melt butter in small saucepan over low
     heat.
· Add crab meat to saltines.
· Pour melted butter and sherry over crab
     meat mixture.
· Gently stir in chopped vegetables, parsley,
     and pepper.
· Salt to taste.
· Spoon mixture into four large scallop shells
     or spread evenly into a shallow 9-inch-
     square casserole.
· Bake shells for 20 minutes (casserole for 30
     minutes).

MOUSSE OF SOLE

(Serves 4)

INGREDIENTS

1½	pounds fillet of sole
1	tablespoon unsalted butter, softened
1½	cups heavy cream
1	teaspoon salt
⅛	teaspoon cayenne pepper
3	egg whites

Suggested Sauces

Nantua
Hollandaise
Mousseline
White Wine

HOW TO PROCEED

· Wash fish under cold running water.
· Pat dry with paper towels.
· Grease 6-cup ring mold with butter.
· Assemble ingredients and prepare sauce of
   your choice.
· Cut fillet of sole into 1-inch pieces and blend
   in electric blender ½ cup at a time.*
· Place puréed fish in large bowl.
· Refrigerate for 1 hour, or until very cold.

· Preheat oven to 350° F.

*When using food processor, purée *all* the sole at
one time. Immediately after fish has been puréed,
add cream, salt, and pepper. Scrape fish mixture
into large bowl and refrigerate while beating egg
whites.

- When fish is very cold, beat in heavy cream, about 3 to 4 tablespoons at a time.
- Beat in salt and cayenne pepper.
- Place egg whites in medium-size bowl and beat until soft peaks form.

- Mix one-third egg whites into fish mixture.
- Fold remaining egg whites into mixture until well blended.

- Spoon into mold and smooth top with spatula.
- Place sheet of buttered waxed paper on top, buttered side down.
- Bake in pan of hot water for about 20 minutes, or until mousse puffs up above sides of mold and an inserted knife comes out clean.

· To serve mousse: place on counter top; wipe mold dry; place serving plate on top of mold.

· Quickly turn mold and plate over. Mousse will slide out of mold.
· With paper towel, draw off liquid that has accumulated on serving plate before pouring sauce over mousse.

STEAMING

CLAMS

(Serves 4)

INGREDIENTS

8   dozen soft-shell clams (steamer clams)
        in their shells
½   cup chopped celery leaves
¾   pound (3 sticks) unsalted butter
1   cup water
    salt and pepper

HOW TO PROCEED

· Wash clams under cold running water to
    remove sand.
· Scatter celery leaves on bottom of kettle
    large enough to hold clams.
· Melt butter and keep warm.
· Place clams on top of celery leaves and pour
    in water.
· Place on high heat and bring to a boil.
· Cover tightly and steam clams for 8 to 10
    minutes, or until shells open.
· Discard those that do not open.
· Divide clams evenly among four large soup
    bowls.
· Strain broth through sieve lined with dou-
    ble thickness of cheesecloth.
· Taste broth for salt and pepper.
· Serve broth in coffee mugs.

HOW TO EAT STEAMED CLAMS
· Separate shell with fingers.
· Take clam by neck and pull it loose from
    shell.
· Hold neck of clam with one hand, body with
    the other, and pull sheath from neck of
    clam. Discard sheath.
· Hold clam by neck and dip into melted but-
    ter.
· Sip broth while eating clams.

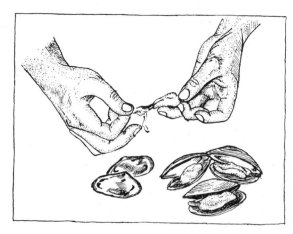

OYSTERS

(Serves 4)

INGREDIENTS

2   dozen oysters, in their shells
4   tablespoons unsalted butter
½   cup finely chopped onions
½   teaspoon freshly ground black pepper
1   cup dry white wine
½   cup water
    salt
½   cup chopped parsley

HOW TO PROCEED

· Wash oysters under cold running water to
    remove sand.
· Melt butter in 8- to 10-quart pot over me-
    dium to high heat.
· When butter is very hot and stops bubbling,
    add onions and cook, stirring all the
    while, for 3 to 4 minutes.
· Add pepper, wine, and water.
· Bring liquid to a boil. Add oysters.
· Bring liquid back to a boil, cover pot, and
    reduce heat.
· Steam oysters for about 10 minutes, or until
    shells open.
· Remove opened oysters with slotted spoon
    to warm soup plates.
· Discard oysters that have not opened.
· Taste broth for salt, add chopped parsley,
    and pour over oysters.

MUSSELS

(Serves 4)

INGREDIENTS

4   pounds large mussels, in their shells
4   tablespoons unsalted butter
½   cup finely chopped onions
½   teaspoon dried thyme
½   teaspoon freshly ground black pepper
1   cup dry white wine
½   cup water
      salt
¼   cup chopped parsley

HOW TO PROCEED

TO CLEAN MUSSELS
· First remove hairlike beard by pulling it
   from shell.
· Scrub mussels under cold running water
   with copper or wire brush. Remove all sea
   growth with sharp knife.

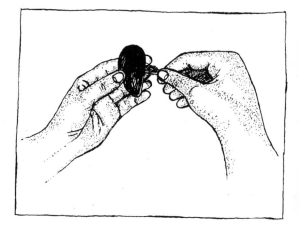

· Melt butter in 8- to 10-quart pot over me-
   dium-high heat.
· When butter is very hot and stops bubbling,
   add onions and cook, stirring all the
   while, for 3 to 4 minutes.
· Add thyme, pepper, white wine, and water.
· Bring liquid to a boil. Add mussels.
· Bring liquid back to a boil, cover pot, reduce
   heat.
· Steam mussels for about 10 minutes, or un-
   til shells open.
· Remove opened mussels to warm soup
   plates with slotted spoon.
· Discard mussels that have not opened.
· Taste broth for salt, add chopped parsley,
   and spoon over mussels.

STUFFED LOBSTER WITH COGNAC

(Serves 4)

INGREDIENTS

4	live lobsters, 1¾ pounds each
1	teaspoon salt
¼	cup fresh bread crumbs
¼	cup freshly grated Parmesan cheese
2	tablespoons chopped parsley
4	tablespoons unsalted butter
¼	cup chopped shallots or scallions
1	cup sliced fresh mushrooms
3	tablespoons flour
1¼	cups light cream
¼	teaspoon cayenne pepper
¼	cup cognac

HOW TO PROCEED

· Place live lobsters on their backs. With kitchen string, tie a long wooden spoon in three or four places along underside of each lobster to keep it from curling.

· Add about 3 inches of water to a pot large enough to hold lobsters (use more than one pot if necessary or cook only two at a time) along with salt.

· Bring to a boil over high heat and add lobsters. When water returns to a boil, reduce heat, cover, and steam for 20 to 22 minutes.

· Remove lobsters from water and let cool to room temperature.

· Remove strings and spoons from lobsters. Twist off antennae and discard.

· Twist off claws and crack them with lobster cracker or cleaver.

· Remove meat from large claws.

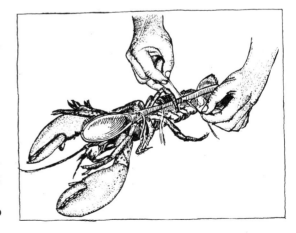

· With sharp knife, cut large opening down
   the back of each lobster.
· Starting from base of head down to middle
   of last section of tail, remove all meat
   from body and tail. Set shells aside.
· Discard coral, sac, and intestinal vein attached to it.
· With small spoon, remove tomalley (liver)
   and reserve.
· Cut all lobster meat into ½-inch pieces.
· Preheat oven to 400° F.
· Mix bread crumbs, cheese, and parsley in
   small bowl.
· Heat butter in heavy skillet over medium
   heat.

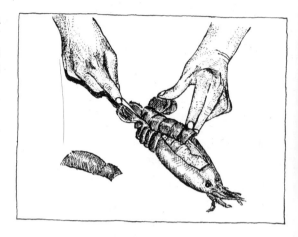

· Cook shallots or scallions in butter for 1
   minute.
· Add mushrooms, and cook for 10 minutes
   more, stirring once or twice.
· Stir in flour and cook for 2 minutes more.
· Beat cream into mixture with wire whisk.
· Bring to a boil and cook until sauce thick-
   ens.
· Reduce heat, add tomalley, remaining 1 tea-
   spoon salt, cayenne pepper, and cognac.
· Simmer sauce over low heat for 3 minutes.
· Remove from heat and stir in lobster meat.
· Divide lobster mixture evenly and stuff
   lobster cavities.
· Sprinkle with bread crumb mixture.
· Place stuffed lobsters on large baking sheet.
· Bake in middle of oven for about 15 min-
   utes, or until stuffing bubbles and top-
   ping turns golden brown.
· Serve immediately.

DEEP-FAT FRYING

DEEP-FRIED FISH IN BATTER

(SOLE, HADDOCK, FLOUNDER, COD, OCEAN PERCH, OR ANY WHITE-MEAT FISH)
(Serves 4)

INGREDIENTS

2   pounds fillet of white-meat fish, cut into
      8-ounce portions
1   lemon

FOR BATTER
1   cup flour
½   teaspoon salt
¾   cup water
3   tablespoons vegetable oil
1   egg white

FOR FRYING
    vegetable oil
1   cup flour

Suggested Sauces

Tartar
Rémoulade

HOW TO PROCEED

· Wash fish under cold running water.
· Pat dry with paper towels.
· Cut lemon into wedges for garnish and set
   aside in refrigerator.

TO MAKE BATTER
· Place 1 cup flour, the salt, water, and 3 tablespoons vegetable oil in large bowl.
· Blend well with wooden spoon.
· If mixture seems thick and holds its shape
   on spoon, stir in up to 2 more tablespoons
   water.
· Beat egg white until it forms soft peaks and
   fold gently into flour mixture.

TO FRY AND FINISH
- Preheat oven to 200° F.
- Pour vegetable oil into electric deep-fat fryer about 4 inches deep and heat to 375° F. Or, fill large cast-iron skillet two-thirds full and heat.
- Place 1 cup flour on large, flat plate.
- Dredge fish first in flour and shake off excess.
- Next dip into batter. Let excess drain back into bowl, leaving only a thin coating on fish.

- Gently place fish in hot oil and fry, two or three pieces at a time, turning once or twice, until golden brown, about 3 to 4 minutes.
- Remove with slotted spoon and drain on paper towels.
- Keep warm in oven until all fish is fried.
- Serve with lemon wedges and sauce of your choice.

BATTER-FRIED SHRIMP

(Serves 4)

INGREDIENTS

2   dozen jumbo shrimp, peeled and
         deveined, with tails left on (see p. 6
         for how to peel and devein shrimp)

FOR DIPPING SAUCE
½   cup Japanese soy sauce
2   tablespoons dry sherry
1   cup chicken broth
3   tablespoons prepared horseradish

FOR BATTER
1½   cups flour
1   teaspoon baking powder
1   egg yolk
2   cups water

FOR FRYING
        vegetable oil
1   cup flour

HOW TO PROCEED

· With small sharp knife, starting from tail
   section on underside of shrimp, slice
   length of shrimp to the other end without
   cutting all the way through, leaving a
   hinge about ⅛ inch thick.

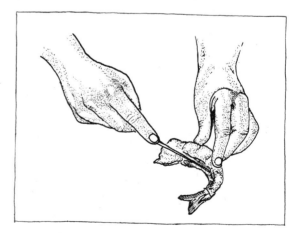

· Place shrimp, cut side up, and make criss-cross cuts in the flesh.
· Wash shrimp in cold running water and pat dry with paper towels.

TO MAKE DIPPING SAUCE
· Combine all ingredients for dipping sauce.
· Cover and set aside.

TO MAKE BATTER
· Sift the 1½ cups flour with the baking powder.
· Beat egg yolk and water together and add to flour gradually, stirring until batter is smooth.

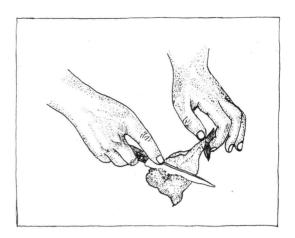

TO FRY AND FINISH
· Preheat oven to 200° F.
· Fill large cast-iron skillet two-thirds full with vegetable oil and heat. Or, pour oil into electric deep-fat fryer about 4 inches deep and heat to 375° F.
· Place 1 cup flour on large, flat plate.
· Dredge shrimp in flour and shake off excess.
· Holding shrimp by tail, dip into batter. Let excess drain back into bowl, leaving only a thin coating on shrimp.
· Gently place shrimp in hot oil, four to six at a time, and fry, turning once or twice, until golden brown, about 2 to 3 minutes.
· Remove with slotted spoon and drain on paper towels.
· Keep warm in oven until all shrimp are fried.
· Serve with dipping sauce.

OYSTERS IN BATTER

(Serves 4)

INGREDIENTS

32 shucked oysters (see p. 10 for how to
    shuck oysters)
1   lemon

FOR BATTER
1   cup flour
½   teaspoon salt
¾   cup water
3   tablespoons vegetable oil
1   egg white

FOR FRYING
    vegetable oil
1   cup flour

Suggested Sauces

Tartar
Rémoulade

HOW TO PROCEED

· Thread four oysters, one at a time, onto
    bamboo skewers.
· Cut lemon into wedges for garnish and set
    aside in refrigerator.

TO MAKE BATTER
· Place 1 cup flour, the salt, water, and veg-
    etable oil in large bowl.
· Stir with wooden spoon to blend well.
· If mixture seems thick and holds its shape
    on spoon, stir in up to 2 more tablespoons
    water.
· In large bowl beat egg white to form soft
    peaks and fold thoroughly into flour mix-
    ture.

TO FRY AND FINISH

· Preheat oven to 200° F.
· Fill large cast-iron skillet two-thirds full
    with vegetable oil and heat. Or, pour oil
    into deep-fat fryer about 4 inches deep
    and heat to 375° F.
· Place 1 cup flour on large, flat plate.
· Dredge skewered oysters in flour and shake
    off excess.
· Dip oysters into batter. Let excess batter
    drain back into the bowl, leaving only a
    thin coating on oysters.
· Using a large two-prong fork, gently place
    oysters in hot fat. Fry skewered oysters
    three or four at a time until golden
    brown, about 3 minutes.
· Remove with slotted spoon and drain on pa-
    per towels.
· Keep warm in oven until all oysters are
    fried.
· Serve with lemon wedges and sauce of your
    choice.

CODFISH BALLS

(Serves 4)

INGREDIENTS

1   pound salt cod
1½   pounds potatoes (about 5 medium-size)
1   teaspoon salt
6   tablespoons unsalted butter
1   egg
1   teaspoon Worcestershire sauce
¼   teaspoon cayenne pepper
      vegetable oil

Suggested Sauces

Tartar
Rémoulade

HOW TO PROCEED

· The night before you are planning to serve, place cod in large bowl, cover with cold water, and soak overnight.

· Drain cod and place in saucepan; cover with fresh cold water.
· Bring water to a boil over high heat; reduce heat to simmer. Cook cod for 20 to 30 minutes, or until cod flakes easily when tested with a fork.
· Meanwhile, peel potatoes and place in saucepan; cover with cold water; add salt.
· Bring water to a boil; reduce heat to simmer.
· Cook potatoes until tender, about 20 minutes.
· Drain water from potatoes and cook over high heat, shaking pan, until potatoes are dry.

· While potatoes are still warm, purée them
   in a food mill or push them through a
   ricer.
· When cod is cool, flake with your fingers,
   removing bones and any pieces of skin.
· Beat cod flakes, butter, egg, Worcestershire
   sauce, and cayenne pepper into potato
   purée.

· Shape mixture into 1½-inch balls.
· Preheat oven to 200° F.
· Fill large cast-iron skillet two-thirds full
   with vegetable oil and heat. Or, pour oil
   into deep-fat fryer about 4 inches deep
   and heat to 375° F.
· Gently place six to eight codfish balls in hot
   oil and fry until golden brown, about 3
   minutes.
· Remove with slotted spoon and drain on paper towels.
· Keep warm in oven until all codfish balls
   are fried.
· Serve with sauce of your choice.

SOFT-SHELL CRABS

(Serves 4)

INGREDIENTS

4   large (or 8 medium-size) soft-shell crabs
1   tablespoon salt
2   lemons
    vegetable oil
4   eggs
1   cup flour
2½ cups fresh bread crumbs

Suggested Sauces

Tartar
Rémoulade

HOW TO PROCEED

· Wash crabs under cold running water. Remove seaweed that still clings.
· With a sharp knife, remove apron-shaped flap from underside of crab.

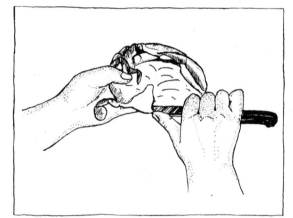

· Turn crab and lift pointed shell first on one side, then on other, and scrape out spongy lungs.

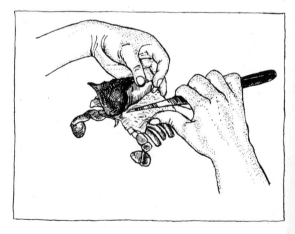

· With scissors, sever head behind eyes and
   press crab to eject sand sac from head
   opening.
· Pat crabs dry with paper towels.
· Sprinkle with salt.
· Cut lemons into four wedges each for garnish and set aside in refrigerator.

· Preheat oven to 200° F.
· Fill large cast-iron skillet two-thirds full
   with vegetable oil and heat. Or, pour oil
   into electric deep-fat fryer about 4 inches
   deep and heat to 375° F.

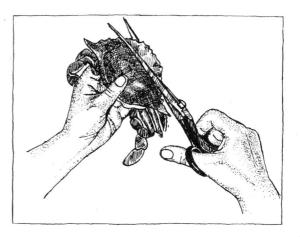

· Beat eggs in shallow dish until well
   blended.
· Place flour on large, flat plate.
· Dredge each crab in flour and shake off excess.
· Then dip in beaten egg, using large fork or
   slotted metal spatula.
· Cover both sides with bread crumbs.
· Gently place at one time, as many crabs as
   will not touch in oil. (To guard against
   splatter, skillet should be partially covered.)
· Fry crabs about 3 to 4 minutes, turning
   once, until golden brown.
· Remove with slotted spoon and drain on paper towels.
· Keep warm in oven until all crabs are fried.
· Serve with lemon wedges and sauce of your
   choice.

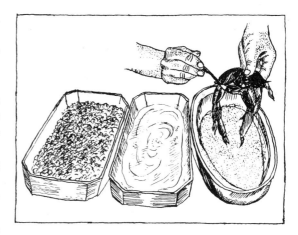

SAUTÉING

CRAB MEAT SAUTÉ

(Serves 4)

INGREDIENTS

1½ pounds fresh lump crab meat or 1½
       pounds frozen king crab meat, thawed
¼   pound (1 stick) unsalted butter
½   teaspoon salt
¼   teaspoon freshly ground black pepper
2   teaspoons Worcestershire sauce
2   tablespoons chopped chives
2   tablespoons chopped parsley
1   lemon

HOW TO PROCEED

· Flake crab meat and remove any cartilage.

· In large skillet, heat butter over medium-
    high heat until very hot.
· Add crab meat and stir with slotted spoon
    until heated through.
· Stir in salt, pepper, Worcestershire sauce,
    chives, and parsley.
· Serve with lemon, cut into wedges.

SCAMPI

(Serves 4)

INGREDIENTS

2   dozen shrimp, in their shells
½   teaspoon salt
1   lemon
4   tablespoons chopped parsley
6   tablespoons unsalted butter
2   tablespoons olive oil
1½ teaspoons finely chopped garlic
¼   teaspoon dried oregano
¼   cup dry white wine

HOW TO PROCEED

· Wash shrimp under cold running water.
· Pat dry with paper towels.
· Place shrimp on its side, with back facing
    you.
· With small sharp knife, cut through shell
    down the back to tail section, leaving a
    hinge about ⅛ inch thick.
· Sprinkle flesh of shrimp with salt.
· Cut lemon into four wedges for garnish.
· Dip wedges into chopped parsley, reserving
    whatever parsley remains, and set aside
    in refrigerator.

· In large skillet, heat butter and oil until
   very hot.
· Add shrimp and stir with large spoon, shak-
   ing pan at the same time.
· Cook shrimp 2 to 3 minutes and turn.
· Cook an additional 2 to 3 minutes or until
   shells are pink and flesh is firm.
· Add chopped garlic and oregano.
· Stir, shaking pan again.
· Cook for 1 minute longer.
· Stir in white wine and sprinkle with re-
   maining chopped parsley.
· Serve with lemon wedges.

CRAB CAKES

(Serves 4)

INGREDIENTS

1 pound fresh lump crab meat or 1 pound
    frozen king crab meat, thawed
1 lemon
1 cup milk
4 tablespoons unsalted butter
1 cup flour
1 teaspoon salt
½ teaspoon white pepper
¼ teaspoon Tabasco sauce
½ cup chopped scallions
¼ cup chopped flat-leaf parsley
4 eggs
2½ cups fresh bread crumbs
1 cup vegetable oil

Suggested Sauces

Tartar
Rémoulade

HOW TO PROCEED

· Flake crab meat into bowl and remove any
   cartilage.
· Cut lemon into four wedges for garnish and
   store in refrigerator.
· Heat milk in small saucepan until small
   bubbles form around edge of pan.
· Melt butter in heavy saucepan, add 4 tablespoons flour, and cook over low heat, stirring with wooden spoon for 2 minutes.
· Remove pan from heat; with wire whisk,
   beat hot milk slowly into flour-butter
   mixture.
· Add salt, pepper, and Tabasco sauce.
· Return mixture to high heat and continue
   to beat with whisk until sauce comes to
   a boil.
· Reduce heat, and let sauce simmer for 2
   minutes.
· Remove from heat and pour sauce over crab
   meat.
· Stir in scallions and parsley.

· Spread crab meat mixture into shallow dish.
· Refrigerate for 1 hour.

· Divide chilled crab meat mixture into eight
    equal portions.
· Shape crab cakes ¾ inch thick and 3 inches
    in diameter.
· Beat eggs in shallow dish until well
    blended.

· Dredge each crab cake in the remaining
    flour and shake off excess. Using slotted
    metal spatula, coat with beaten egg first,
    then with bread crumbs.
· Preheat oven to 200° F.
· Place oil in heavy cast-iron skillet over me-
    dium-high heat.
· Sauté crab cakes in hot oil for 2 to 3 min-
    utes, then fry on other side, until golden
    brown.
· Remove with slotted spoon and drain on pa-
    per towels.
· Keep warm in oven until all crab cakes are
    sautéed.
· Serve with lemon wedges and sauce of your
    choice.

SOLE MEUNIÈRE

(ALSO FLOUNDER OR OCEAN PERCH)
(Serves 4)

INGREDIENTS

1 to 2½ pounds fillets of sole
½   teaspoon salt
1   lemon
½   cup flour
½   pound (2 sticks) unsalted butter
2   tablespoons chopped parsley

HOW TO PROCEED

· Wash fish under cold running water.
· Pat dry with paper towels.
· Sprinkle with salt.
· Cut lemon into four wedges for garnish and
    store in refrigerator.
· Preheat oven to 200° F.
· Place flour on large, flat plate.
· Dredge fillets in flour and shake off excess.
· Heat 1 stick of butter in large skillet.
· When butter is hot and bubbling, place
    floured fish in skillet.
· Shake skillet gently once or twice to insure
    that fish does not stick.
· Sauté fish for 2 to 3 minutes.
· Using two spatulas, gently turn fish over
    and shake pan again.
· Cook for 2 to 3 minutes more, or until fish
    flakes easily when tested with a fork.
· Transfer to warm serving platter.
· Pour hot butter from pan over fish.
· Keep fish warm in oven until all fillets are
    sautéed.
· Wipe skillet clean with paper towels.
· Return skillet to heat and add remaining
    stick of butter.
· Cook remaining fish in the same manner.
· Sprinkle with chopped parsley.
· Serve with lemon wedges.

BROOK TROUT AMANDINE

(Serves 4)

INGREDIENTS

4   brook trout, 10 to 12 ounces each
1   teaspoon salt
¼   teaspoon pepper
1   lemon
1½ cups flour
½   pound (2 sticks) unsalted butter
1   cup sliced blanched almonds
2   tablespoons lemon juice
2   tablespoons dry white wine
2   tablespoons chopped parsley

HOW TO PROCEED

· Wash trout under cold running water.
· Pat dry with paper towels.
· Sprinkle with salt and pepper.
· Cut lemon into four wedges for garnish and
    set aside in refrigerator.
· Place flour on large, flat plate.
· Dredge trout in flour and shake off excess.

· Heat 1 stick of butter in large skillet.
· When butter is hot and bubbling, place
    floured fish in skillet.
· Shake skillet gently once or twice to insure
    that fish does not stick.
· Sauté for 5 minutes.

· Using two spatulas, gently turn fish over
   and shake skillet again.
· Cook for 5 minutes more.
· Transfer fish to warm serving platter.
· Discard butter and wipe skillet clean with
   paper towels.
· Return skillet to heat, melt remaining stick
   of butter.
· When butter starts to bubble, add almonds.
· Sauté almonds, stirring with large spoon 2
   or 3 minutes or until they turn light
   brown.
· Stir in lemon juice and white wine and re-
   move from heat immediately.

· Spoon mixture over trout.
· Sprinkle with chopped parsley.
· Serve with lemon wedges.

SOFT-SHELL CRABS MEUNIÈRE

(Serves 4)

INGREDIENTS

1   dozen small soft-shell crabs
2   teaspoons salt
2   lemons
1½ sticks unsalted butter
4   tablespoons vegetable oil
1½ cups flour
4   tablespoons chopped parsley

HOW TO PROCEED

· Wash crabs under cold running water and
    remove seaweed that still clings.
· With sharp knife, remove apron-shaped flap
    from underside of crab.

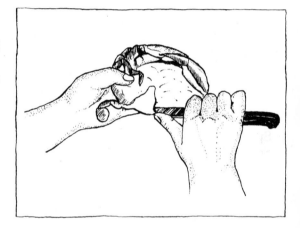

· Turn crab and lift pointed shell first on one
    side, then on other, and scrape out spongy
    lungs.

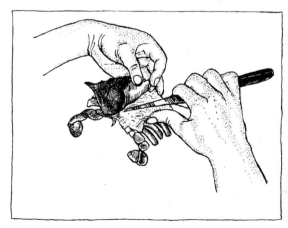

· With scissors, sever head behind eyes and
  press crab to eject sand sac from head
  opening.
· Pat crabs dry with paper towels.
· Sprinkle with salt.
· Cut lemons into four wedges each for garnish and set aside in refrigerator.

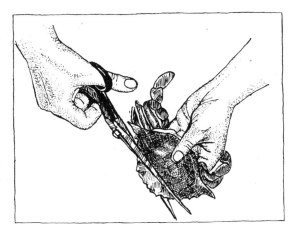

· Preheat oven to 200° F.
· Put butter and oil in large skillet; heat over
  moderate heat until butter starts to bub-
  ble.
· Place flour on large, flat plate.
· Dredge crabs in flour and shake off excess.
· Sauté crabs, four at a time, for 5 minutes.
  (To guard against splatter, skillet should
  be partially covered.)
· Turn two or three times, or until edges are
  crisp. Adjust heat to keep butter from
  burning.
· Remove crabs to platter and keep warm in
  oven while sautéing the remaining crabs.
· Sprinkle with parsley.
· Serve with lemon wedges.

SCALLOPS PROVENÇALE

(Serves 4)

INGREDIENTS

2   pounds bay scallops
1   lemon
¾   pound (3 sticks) unsalted butter, melted
½   teaspoon salt
¼   teaspoon freshly ground pepper
½   cup flour
2   teaspoons finely chopped garlic
2   tablespoons chopped parsley

HOW TO PROCEED

· Four to 6 hours before cooking, place scallops on jelly-roll pan lined with paper towels.
· Place another layer of towels on top of scallops. Store in refrigerator.
· Cut lemon into four wedges and store in refrigerator.
· Melt butter over low heat and set aside.
· With small spoon, remove and discard foam from melted butter, draw off clear butter fat, avoiding any milky substance that has settled. Reserve.
· Preheat oven to 200° F.
· Just before cooking, sprinkle scallops with salt and pepper.
· Place flour on large, flat pan.
· Dredge scallops in flour.

· Place them in large wire strainer and shake
    to remove excess flour.
· Place large skillet on high heat and add half
    the butter.
· When butter is very hot and just starts to
    smoke, carefully add half the floured
    scallops.
· Stir scallops with large slotted spoon, shak-
    ing pan at the same time.
· Cook scallops for 2 to 3 minutes.
· Add half the chopped garlic; stir, and shake
    pan again.
· Cook for 1 minute more.

· Divide scallops among two scallop shells.
· Place in oven to keep warm.
· Wipe pan clean with paper towels.
· Cook remaining scallops in same fashion.
· Sprinkle scallops with chopped parsley.
· Serve with lemon wedges.

POACHING

CODFISH, HADDOCK, OR SALMON STEAKS

(Serves 4)

INGREDIENTS

4   codfish, haddock, or salmon steaks,
        8 ounces each

FOR POACHING LIQUID
1   cup dry white wine
4   cups water
1   carrot, sliced
1   cup chopped onions
6   peppercorns
1   sprig parsley
¼   teaspoon dried thyme
1   tablespoon salt

Suggested Sauces

For codfish or haddock

Mustard Sauce
Egg and Tomato Sauce

For salmon

Béarnaise
Hollandaise
Mousseline

HOW TO PROCEED

· Combine ingredients for poaching liquid in
    shallow saucepan large enough to hold
    four fish steaks and bring to a boil.
· Remove from heat and let cool to room tem-
    perature.
· Assemble ingredients and prepare sauce of
    your choice.
· Wash fish under cold running water.
· Wrap each steak in cheesecloth and tie both
    ends with string.
· Place fish in cooled poaching liquid.
· Bring liquid to a simmer over medium heat,
    cover, and poach fish for 6 to 8 minutes,
    or until it flakes easily when tested with
    a fork.
· Remove fish from liquid with large, slotted
    spatula.
· Cut cheesecloth loose and place fish on serv-
    ing platter.
· Use paper towels to draw off any liquid that
    has accumulated on platter.
· Spoon sauce over fish before serving.

STRIPED BASS

(Serves 4)

INGREDIENTS

2½ to 3 pounds striped bass, cleaned, with
    head and tail left on

FOR POACHING LIQUID
6   cups water
2   cups dry white wine
1   carrot, sliced
1   cup chopped onions
6 to 8 peppercorns
2   sprigs parsley
¼   teaspoon dried thyme
3   tablespoons salt

Suggested Sauces

White Wine
Hollandaise
Mousseline
Sauce Beurre Blanc

HOW TO PROCEED

· Combine ingredients for poaching liquid in
   large fish poacher and bring to a boil.
· Remove from heat and let cool to room temperature.
· Assemble ingredients and prepare sauce of
   your choice.
· Wash fish inside and out under cold running
   water.
· Wrap fish in cheesecloth and tie both ends
   with string.

· Place fish in cooled poaching liquid and tie
   string ends to handles of poacher. Liquid
   should cover fish. If not, add water.

· Bring liquid to a simmer over medium heat, cover, and poach fish for 20 minutes or until it flakes easily when tested with a fork.
· Remove fish to serving platter with two spatulas.

· Open cheesecloth, and with small knife, remove skin, starting from base of tail all the way to gill.
· Using cheesecloth as an aid, turn fish over, and remove skin on other side.
· Discard cheesecloth.
· Use paper towels to draw off any liquid that has accumulated on platter.
· Spoon sauce over fish before serving.

OCEAN PERCH FLORENTINE

(Serves 4)

INGREDIENTS

4   fillets of ocean perch, 8 ounces each
3   tablespoons unsalted butter, softened
¼   cup chopped scallions
¼   cup clam juice
¼   cup dry white wine
1   bay leaf

FOR SAUCE
1   cup milk
3   tablespoons unsalted butter
1   tablespoon chopped onions
4   tablespoons flour
½   teaspoon salt
⅛   teaspoon cayenne pepper
¼   teaspoon nutmeg
⅛   teaspoon dried thyme
2   tablespoons grated Parmesan cheese

2   packages frozen spinach, 10 ounces each
¼   cup grated Swiss cheese

HOW TO PROCEED

· Preheat oven to 350° F.
· Place fillets skin side down on chopping
    board.
· To skin, with sharp, heavy knife, cut
    through flesh to the skin ½ inch from tail
    end.
· While holding skin, push knife forward,
    pressing against board and separating
    flesh from skin.
· Grease shallow baking dish (large enough
    to hold four fillets) with 1 tablespoon soft-
    ened butter.
· Scatter scallions over bottom of dish.

- Place skinned fillets on top of scallions in baking dish.
- Pour clam juice and white wine over fillets.
- Place bay leaf on top.
- Cut piece of waxed paper 2 inches longer than baking dish and butter with 1 tablespoon of softened butter.
- Place waxed paper on top of baking dish, buttered side down.
- Place on middle rack of oven and poach for 12 to 14 minutes, or until fish flakes easily when tested with a fork.

TO MAKE SAUCE
- Heat milk in saucepan until small bubbles form around edge of pan.
- Melt 3 tablespoons butter in heavy saucepan, and cook onions in butter over medium heat for 1 to 2 minutes.
- Add flour and cook over low heat, stirring with wooden spoon for 2 minutes.
- Remove pan from heat, and with wire whisk beat hot milk slowly into flour mixture.
- Add salt, cayenne pepper, nutmeg, and thyme.
- Return mixture to heat, and continue to beat with whisk until sauce comes to a boil.
- Reduce heat and let simmer for 2 minutes.
- Remove from heat and set aside.

- When fish is baked, pour about ¾ cup liquid from baking dish into small saucepan.
- Cook over high heat until liquid reduces to ¼ cup.
- Beat reduced liquid into sauce and strain into small bowl.
- Add Parmesan cheese.

FOR FINISHING FISH
- Cook spinach as directed on package.
- Squeeze spinach dry by placing in strainer and pushing it with back of wooden spoon.

- Remove fish from baking dish and set aside.
- Wash and butter baking dish (or butter a second baking dish if available) with remaining tablespoon softened butter.
- Discard bay leaf and any scallions sticking to dish.
- Raise oven heat to 425° F.
- Cover bottom of baking dish with cooked spinach.
- Place fillets on top of spinach.
- Pour sauce over fillets and sprinkle with Swiss cheese.
- Bake for 6 to 8 minutes, or until sauce is bubbly and cheese has melted.
- Serve immediately in baking dish.

SAUCES

AÏOLI

(Makes about 2 cups)

INGREDIENTS

2   cups Mayonnaise (see p. 72)
1   tablespoon finely chopped garlic

HOW TO PROCEED

· Combine ingredients in medium-size bowl,
     mixing well.
· Cover and place in refrigerator for at least
     2 hours before serving.

SAUCE BÉARNAISE

(Makes about 2 cups)

INGREDIENTS

2   cups Sauce Hollandaise (see p. 71)
½   cup white wine vinegar
¼   cup chopped shallots
3½   teaspoons dried tarragon
8   peppercorns, crushed
4   large sprigs parsley
2   tablespoons chopped parsley
     salt and cayenne pepper

HOW TO PROCEED

· Prepare Hollandaise sauce and keep warm.
· Place vinegar, shallots, 2 teaspoons tarra-
     gon, peppercorns, and parsley sprigs in
     small saucepan.
· Bring ingredients in saucepan to a boil over
     high heat.

· Cook until liquid in pan is reduced to about
    2 tablespoons.
· Remove from heat and strain into small
    bowl, pressing with wooden spoon to ex-
    tract all liquid.
· Beat reduced vinegar into Hollandaise
    sauce.
· Add remaining 1½ teaspoons tarragon and
    chopped parsley.
· Taste for salt and cayenne pepper.

CURRY SAUCE

(Makes about 2 cups)

INGREDIENTS

1	teaspoon cumin seeds
1	teaspoon mustard seeds
1	teaspoon peppercorns
½	teaspoon dried red pepper flakes
1	teaspoon coriander seeds
4	large ripe tomatoes (about 2½ pounds)
4	tablespoons unsalted butter
½	cup chopped onions
¼	cup chopped scallions
1	teaspoon turmeric
½	teaspoon salt
2	teaspoons ground ginger
1	cup Fish Stock (see p. 70) or chicken broth

HOW TO PROCEED

· Place cumin seeds, mustard seeds, pepper-
    corns, red pepper flakes, and coriander
    seeds in electric blender and blend for 30
    seconds, or until spices are pulverized.
· In large saucepan, bring 2 quarts water to
    a boil.

· Plunge tomatoes into boiling water, turn off
   heat, and let sit for 30 seconds. Remove
   with slotted spoon.

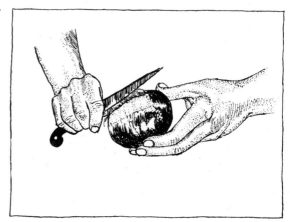

· When tomatoes have cooled, peel with a
   small knife and remove stem end.
· Quarter tomatoes.

· With thumb, remove seeds and discard.
· Finely chop tomatoes and place them in
   small bowl.
· Heat butter in large skillet and sauté onions
   until transparent.
· Stir in scallions.
· Add contents of blender, plus turmeric, salt,
   and ginger, and cook for 2 or 3 minutes
   over low heat.
· Add chopped tomatoes and turn heat up to
   high.
· Cook tomatoes until all water has been
   cooked out, or until mixture resembles
   tomato purée.
· Add fish stock or chicken broth and bring to
   a boil.
· Reduce heat and simmer sauce for 3 to 4
   minutes.

EGG AND TOMATO SAUCE

(Makes about 2 cups)

INGREDIENTS

2   eggs, hard-cooked
2   medium-size ripe tomatoes
¼   pound (1 stick) unsalted butter
¼   cup strained poaching liquid from
        codfish or haddock
½   teaspoon dried dillweed
2   tablespoons chopped chives
½   teaspoon salt
¼   teaspoon freshly ground black pepper
2   tablespoons finely chopped parsley

HOW TO PROCEED

· Chop eggs coarsely and place in small bowl.
· Plunge tomatoes into boiling water, turn off
    heat, and let sit for 30 seconds. Remove
    with slotted spoon.
· When tomatoes have cooled, peel with a
    small knife and remove stem end.
· Quarter tomatoes.
· With thumb, remove seeds and discard.
· Coarsely chop tomatoes and add to chopped
    eggs.
· Melt butter in medium-size saucepan over
    low heat.
· Add strained poaching liquid, eggs, toma-
    toes, dillweed, chives, salt, and pepper.
· Increase heat to medium-high and cook un-
    til sauce is very hot.
· Stir in chopped parsley and serve from
    sauceboat.

FISH STOCK

(Makes about 6 cups)

INGREDIENTS

2   pounds fish trimmings (heads and
         bones)
6   cups water
1   cup dry white wine
1   cup coarsely chopped onions
½   cup chopped celery
1   bay leaf
½   teaspoon dried thyme
1   teaspoon salt
6   peppercorns
1   small carrot, sliced
1   sprig parsley

HOW TO PROCEED

· Wash fish trimmings under cold running
    water until free of bloody particles.
· Line sieve with double thickness of damp-
    ened cheesecloth.
· Place trimmings on chopping board, and
    with a cleaver, chop them into 2-inch
    pieces.
· Place trimmings in large pot and pour water
    and wine over them.
· Add more water if needed to cover.
· Bring liquid to a simmer over medium heat
    and cook for 5 minutes.
· With a slotted spoon, skim off foam as it
    rises to the top.
· Add remaining ingredients and partially
    cover pan.
· Continue to simmer stock for 30 minutes.
· Strain stock through lined sieve into a large
    bowl.
· Fish stock may be refrigerated for three or
    four days or frozen for up to three
    months.

HERBED BUTTER

(Makes about ½ cup)

INGREDIENTS

¼ pound (1 stick) unsalted butter, softened
2 tablespoons chopped parsley
½ teaspoon dried oregano
1 teaspoon Worcestershire sauce
½ teaspoon salt
½ teaspoon freshly ground black pepper
½ teaspoon chopped garlic

HOW TO PROCEED

· In small bowl, mash butter with wooden spoon until soft.
· Mix in above ingredients.
· Chill, then shape butter mixture into roll 1 inch in diameter and about 7 inches long.
· Wrap in waxed paper, return to refrigerator, and chill for about 1 hour or until very firm.

SAUCE HOLLANDAISE

(Makes about 2 cups)

INGREDIENTS

4 egg yolks
1 tablespoon cold water
2 tablespoons lemon juice
½ teaspoon salt
⅛ teaspoon cayenne pepper
½ pound (2 sticks) unsalted butter, melted

HOW TO PROCEED

· Mix all the above ingredients, except butter, in a small heavy saucepan.
· Place saucepan on lowest heat possible and with wire whisk beat until bottom of pan shows through when whisk is drawn across it. Remove from heat.
· Add hot butter, about ¼ cup at a time, beating well after each addition. When all the butter has been incorporated, the sauce will finally hold its shape on a spoon.

TO RECONSTITUTE CURDLED HOLLANDAISE SAUCE
· Over low heat, bring the curdled sauce to a temperature of approximately 140°, almost hot. Turn off the heat and let rest for about 30 minutes. The butter will separate from the solids. With a small ladle, skim off as much of the liquid butter as you can, place into a small dish, and set aside. Over very low heat, place 1 tablespoon of hot water into a saucepan (not aluminum). With a wire whisk, beat the solid part of the sauce into the water, 1 tablespoon at a time, until it is well incorporated into the water. Next, stir in the liquid butter you previously set aside as though you were making the Hollandaise sauce anew.

MAYONNAISE

(Makes about 2 cups)

INGREDIENTS

3	egg yolks, at room temperature
1	teaspoon dry mustard
½	teaspoon salt
½	teaspoon white pepper
1	cup olive oil
½	cup vegetable oil
4	teaspoons lemon juice

HOW TO PROCEED

· Place egg yolks, dry mustard, salt, and pep-
    per in large bowl.
· Combine olive oil and vegetable oil in 2-cup
    liquid measuring cup with spout.
· With electric mixer on high speed, beat egg
    yolk mixture for about 3 minutes.
· At medium speed, slowly add oil in very fine
    stream.
· After 1 cup oil has been incorporated, the
    remainder may be added more rapidly.
· Beat in lemon juice.
· Refrigerate covered.

SAUCE MOUSSELINE

(Makes about 2½ cups)

INGREDIENTS

2   cups Sauce Hollandaise (see p. 71)
1   cup heavy cream, chilled
     salt

HOW TO PROCEED

· Prepare Hollandaise sauce and let cool to
    room temperature.
· In small bowl, whip cream until stiff.
· Fold cream into Hollandaise sauce.
· Taste for salt.
· Serve at room temperature.

MUSTARD SAUCE

(Makes about 1½ cups)

INGREDIENTS

1½ cups milk
2   tablespoons unsalted butter
2   tablespoons chopped onions
1   teaspoon dry mustard
3   tablespoons flour
½   teaspoon salt
2   teaspoons prepared mustard

HOW TO PROCEED

· Heat milk in small saucepan until bubbles form around the edge.
· Melt butter in medium-size saucepan over low heat.
· When butter is hot, add onions and cook for 3 minutes.
· Stir in dry mustard and flour.
· Cook over low heat for 2 minutes.
· Remove pan from heat.
· With wire whisk, slowly beat hot milk into flour mixture.
· Add salt and prepared mustard.
· Return mixture to high heat and continue to beat with wire whisk until sauce comes to a boil.
· Reduce heat and let sauce simmer for 2 minutes.
· Strain through a sieve.

SAUCE NANTUA

(Makes about 2 cups)

INGREDIENTS

¼   pound shrimp, in their shells
1½ cups milk
9   tablespoons unsalted butter
¾   cup Fish Stock (see p. 70) or clam juice
1   tablespoon chopped onions
4   tablespoons flour
⅛   teaspoon dried thyme
⅛   teaspoon cayenne pepper
1   teaspoon salt

HOW TO PROCEED

· Wash shrimp under cold running water.
· Cut into ½-inch pieces, shell and all.
· Heat milk in saucepan until small bubbles form around edge of pan.
· Heat 6 tablespoons butter in small skillet over medium heat.
· Cook shrimp in butter until shells turn pink and flesh is firm.
· Scrape shrimp and butter into container of electric blender.
· Add fish stock or clam juice and blend at high speed until shrimp pieces are completely pulverized.
· Scrape contents of blender into wire sieve over medium-size bowl.
· With back of wooden spoon, push mixture through wire sieve, separating shells; discard solids. Refrigerate "shrimp butter."

· Melt remaining 3 tablespoons butter in heavy saucepan; cook onions in butter for 2 minutes over medium heat.
· Add flour, and cook over low heat, stirring with wooden spoon for 2 minutes.
· Remove pan from heat, and with wire whisk, slowly beat hot milk into flour mixture.
· Add thyme and cayenne pepper.
· Return mixture to heat and continue to beat with whisk until sauce comes to a boil.
· Reduce heat and let sauce simmer for 2 minutes.
· Remove from heat and strain into bowl.
· Wash saucepan and return sauce to it.
· Remove "shrimp butter" from refrigerator.
· Place sauce on very low heat, and with wire whisk, beat shrimp mixture into sauce, 1 tablespoon at a time.
· Correct seasoning by adding salt, ¼ teaspoon at a time.

RÉMOULADE

(Makes about 2¼ cups)

INGREDIENTS

2   cups Mayonnaise (see p. 72)
1½   teaspoons finely chopped garlic
1   tablespoon chopped chives
1   teaspoon dried tarragon
1   tablespoon chopped parsley
1   teaspoon chopped capers
1   teaspoon dry mustard
¼   cup chopped gherkins

HOW TO PROCEED

· Combine all ingredients in medium-size
    bowl, mixing well.
· Cover and place in refrigerator for at least
    2 hours before serving.

SAUCE BEURRE BLANC

(WHITE BUTTER SAUCE)
(Makes about 1½ cups)

INGREDIENTS

½   pound (2 sticks) unsalted butter
½   cup white wine vinegar
½   cup dry white wine
¼   cup chopped scallions
½   teaspoon salt
⅛   teaspoon white pepper

HOW TO PROCEED

· Cut butter into quarter-inch cubes. Refrigerate.
· Place remaining ingredients in heavy enameled saucepan.
· Bring ingredients in saucepan to a boil.
· Continue to cook mixture over high heat until liquid reduces to about 2 tablespoons.
· Remove from heat.
· With wire whisk, beat in 3 to 4 tablespoons butter pieces until they are completely incorporated.
· Return pan to low heat and, little by little, incorporate remaining butter in the same way.
· When complete, sauce will have a mayonnaise-like consistency.

TARTAR SAUCE

(Makes about 3 cups)

INGREDIENTS

2   cups Mayonnaise (see p. 72)
½   cup finely grated onion
½   cup finely chopped dill pickle
1   tablespoon finely chopped parsley
½   teaspoon salt
⅛   teaspoon cayenne pepper

HOW TO PROCEED

· Combine all ingredients in medium-size bowl.
· Mix well.
· Refrigerate covered for at least 1 hour before serving.
· Serve chilled.

WHITE WINE SAUCE

(Makes about 2 cups)

INGREDIENTS

2½   cups Fish Stock (see p. 70), heated
2   egg yolks
¼   pound (1 stick) unsalted butter
6   tablespoons flour
1   tablespoon lemon juice
      salt and pepper to taste

HOW TO PROCEED

· Bring fish stock to a boil in saucepan, then
    remove from heat.
· Beat egg yolks in cup until well blended.
· Melt half the butter in heavy saucepan over
    low heat.
· Stir in flour and cook for 1 minute.
· Remove from heat.
· With wire whisk, beat hot fish stock into
    butter and flour mixture.
· Return to burner, increase heat, and bring
    to a boil, whisking all the time.
· Reduce heat to simmer, and cook sauce until
    it is reduced to about 2 cups.
· Remove from heat and beat in egg yolks
    until thoroughly blended.
· Whisk in remaining 4 tablespoons butter 1
    tablespoon at a time.
· Beat in lemon juice.
· Taste for salt and pepper.

Index

Aïoli sauce, 66
Almonds
   in brook trout amandine, 52–53

Baking recipes, 15–26
Batter
   deep-fried fish in, 34–35
   -fried shrimp, 36–37
   oysters in, 38–39
Béarnaise, sauce, 66–67
Bluefish
   baked
      with citrus fruit juices, 17
      with onions and tomatoes, 16
Broiling recipes, 1–14
Brook trout amandine, 52–53
Butter
   herbed, 71
      clams with, 8–9
      oysters with, 10–11
   sauce beurre blanc, 76–77
   sauce Hollandaise, 71–72

Citrus fruit juices, red snapper or bluefish with, 17
Clams
   how to eat, 28
   how to shuck, 8–9
   steamed, 28
   with herbed butter, broiled, 8–9
Codfish
   balls, deep-fried, 40–41
   poached, 60
Crab(s)
   cakes, sautéed, 49–50
   deviled, 23
   how to clean and prepare, 42–43, 54–55
   king crab legs, broiled, 4–5
   meat
      sauté, 46
      striped bass stuffed with, 20
   soft-shell
      deep-fried, 42–43
      Meunière, 54–55
Cream
   sauce Mousseline, 73
Curry sauce, 67–68

Deep-fat frying recipes, 33–43
Deviled crabs, 23

Egg(s)
   mayonnaise, 72–73
   sauce Hollandaise, 71–72
   and tomato sauce, 69–70

Fillet of sole
   how to purée, 24
   Meunière, 51
   mousse of, 24–26
Fish
   deep-fried, in batter, 34–35
   stock, 70
      curry sauce, 67–68
      sauce Nantua, 74–75
      white wine sauce, 78
   teriyaki, broiled, 3
   tips on buying, xiii–xiv
   See also specific types of fish and seafood
Flounder Meunière, 51
Frying recipes, deep-fat, 33–43

Haddock, poached, 60
Herbed butter, 71
   clams with, 8–9
   oysters with, 10–11
Hollandaise, sauce, 71–72
   sauce Béarnaise, 66–67
   sauce Mousseline, 73

King crab legs, broiled, 4–5

Lobster
   how to remove meat from, 31–32
   how to split in half, 12
   stuffed
      with cognac, steamed, 31–32
      with shrimp, broiled, 12–13

Marinade for shrimp on a skewer, 6
Mayonnaise, 72–73
   aïoli, 66
   rémoulade, 76
   tartar sauce, 77
Mousseline, sauce, 73

Mussels
  how to clean, 30
  steamed, 30
Mustard sauce, 74

Nantua, sauce, 74–75

Ocean perch
  Florentine, 63–64
  how to skin, 63
  Meunière, 51
Onions, bluefish or striped bass with tomatoes
      and, 16
Oysters
  how to shuck, 10–11
  in batter, 38–39
  Rockefeller, 21–22
  steamed, 29
  with herbed butter, broiled, 10–11

Poaching recipes, 59–64
Potatoes
  codfish balls, 40–41

Red snapper with citrus fruit juices, baked, 17
Rémoulade, sauce, 76

Salmon steaks
  broiled, 2
  poached, 60
Sauces, 65–78
  aïoli, 66
  Béarnaise, 66–67
  beurre blanc, 76–77
  curry, 67–68
  egg and tomato, 69
  fish stock, 70
  herbed butter, 71
    clams with, 8–9
    oysters with, 10–11
  Hollandaise, 71–72
  mayonnaise, 72–73
  Mousseline, 73
  mustard, 74
  Nantua, 74–75
  for ocean perch Florentine, 63, 64
  rémoulade, 76

tartar, 77
white butter, 76–77
white wine, 78
Sautéing recipes, 45–57
Scallops Provençale, 56–57
Scampi, 47–48
Shrimp
  baked stuffed, 18–19
  batter-fried, 36–37
  how to butterfly, 18
  lobster stuffed with, 12–13
  on a skewer, broiled, 6–7
  removing shell from, 6
  sauce Nantua, 74–75
  scampi, 47–48
Soft-shell crabs
  deep-fried, 42–43
  Meunière, 54–55
Sole
  how to purée, 24
  Meunière, 51
  mousse of, 24–26
Spinach
  in ocean perch Florentine, 63–64
  in oysters Rockefeller, 21–22
Steaming recipes, 27–32
Stock, fish, 70
  curry sauce, 67–68
  sauce Nantua, 74–75
  white wine sauce, 78
Striped bass
  baked
    stuffed, 20
    with onions and tomatoes, 16
  poached, 61–62

Tartar sauce, 77
Teriyaki, fish, 3
Tomato(es)
  bluefish or striped bass with onions and, 16
  curry sauce, 67–68
  and egg sauce, 69
Trout amandine, brook, 52–53

White butter sauce, 76–77
White wine sauce, 78
Wine sauce, white, 78